Papa Noah Built an Ark

C. G. Merrily Traditional American

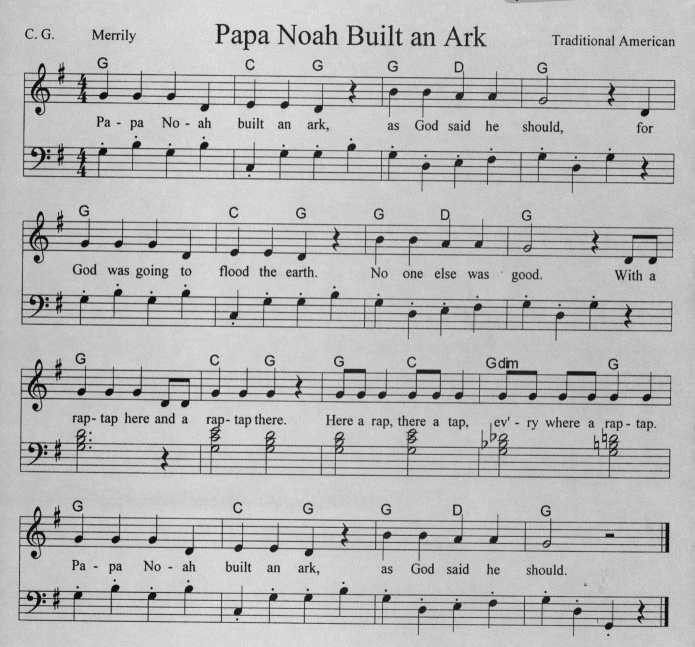

Pa - pa No - ah built an ark, as God said he should, for

God was going to flood the earth. No one else was good. With a

rap-tap here and a rap-tap there. Here a rap, there a tap, ev'-ry where a rap-tap.

Pa - pa No - ah built an ark, as God said he should.

This book is for Tyler and David Tate.

Papa Noah Built an Ark

Carol Greene

Illustrated by Christopher Gray

*The text of this book may be sung to the tune
of "Old MacDonald Had a Farm."*

CPH
SAINT LOUIS

Papa Noah built an ark,
As God said he should,
For God was going
  to flood the earth,
No one else was good.

With a *rap-tap* here
And a *rap-tap* there.
Here a *rap*, there a *tap*,
Everywhere a *rap-tap*.

Papa Noah built an ark,
As God said he should.

Noah's neighbors all made fun.
"My, your boat is grand!
And we can't wait to see you sail
Right here on dry land."

With a *tee-hee* here
And a *tee-hee* there.
Here a *tee*, there a *hee*.
Everywhere a *tee-hee*.

Noah's neighbors all made fun.
"My your boat is grand!"

"Two of every animal
Must go in with you,"
Said God to Noah. "Oh, and yes,
Bring your family too!"

There were *hippos* here,
There were *pandas* there.
Here the *mice,* there the *cats,*
Over there the *wombats.*

"Two of every animal
Must go in with you."

Right into the ark they marched,
Pair by pair by pair.
It seemed as if they knew that God
Wanted each pair there.

With a *stomp-stomp* here
And a *clomp-clomp* there.
Here a *skip*, there a *jump,*
After that a *thump-thump*.

Right into the ark they marched,
Pair by pair by pair.

When the ark was full at last,
God shut its door tight.
And Papa Noah groaned out loud.
"What a noisy sight!"

With a *hee-haw* here
And a *honk-honk* there
Here an *arf*, there a *moo*,
Cockadoodle-*doo-doo*!

When the ark was full at last,
God shut its door tight.

Then the rain came pouring down.
My, how it did pour!
It covered every bit of earth.
Then it poured some more.

With a *drip-drop* here
And a *drip-drop* there.
Here a *drip*, there a *drop*,
Everywhere a *drip-drop*.

Then the rain came pouring down.
My, how it did pour!

All in Papa Noah's ark
Floated safe and sound
For forty days and forty nights,
High above the ground.

With a *splish-splash* here
And a *splish-splash* there.
Here a *splish*, there a *splash*,
Everywhere a *splish-splash*.

All in Papa Noah's ark
Floated safe and sound.

Then God sent a drying wind
Till that big ark sat
Just like a weary, wooden bird
On Mount Ararat.

With a *wooo-eee* here
And a *wooo-eee* there.
Here a *wooo*, there an *eee*,
Everywhere a *wooo-eee*.

Then God sent a drying wind
Till that big ark sat.

To the raven Noah said,
"Fly out. Look around."
But raven flew back every time;
He found no dry ground.

With a *caw-caw* here
And a *caw-caw* there.
Here a *caw*, there a *caw*,
Everywhere a *caw-caw*.

To the raven Noah said,
"Fly out. Look around."

Next a little dove flew out
One time, two times, three.
She brought a fresh green olive leaf.
Then she flew off—free.

With a *coo-coo* here
And a *coo-coo* there.
Here a *coo*, there a *coo*,
Everywhere a *coo-coo*.

Next a little dove flew out
One time, two times, three.

Papa Noah waited till
God gave him the word.
And then he threw the ark door wide.
Out streamed that great herd.

With a *hip-hop* here
And a *flip-flop* there.
Here a *swoop*, there a *pounce*,
Over there a *bounce-bounce*.

Papa Noah waited till
God gave him the word.

Then God said to all the earth,
"See My rainbow sign.
I won't send such a flood again.
All that lives is Mine."

With a *scarlet* here
And a *purple* there.
Here a *gold*, there a *blue*,
Green and *orange* and *pink* too.

Then God said to all the earth,
"See My rainbow sign."

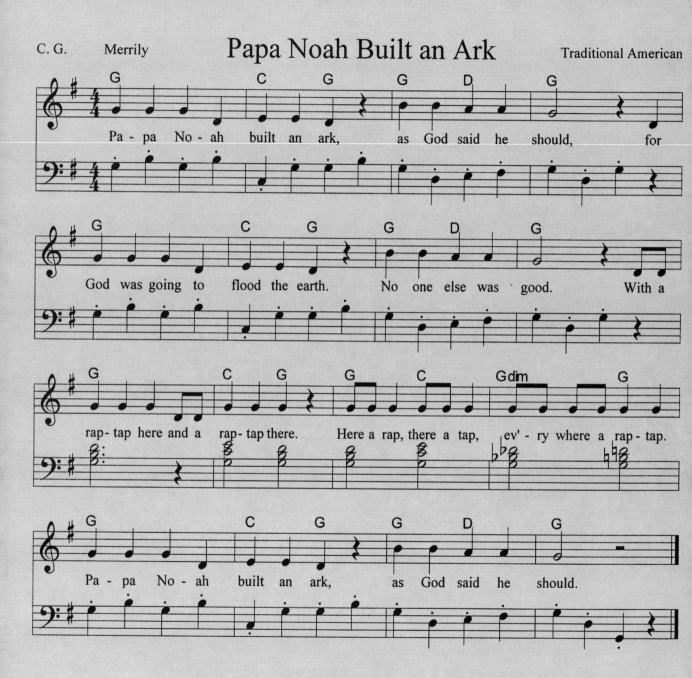

Papa Noah Built an Ark